Quick & Easy

Decorative Painting

Quick & Easy

Decorative Painting

15 step-by-step projects—simple to make, stunning results

STEPHANIE WEIGHTMAN

An imprint of **CREATIVE HOMEOWNER**, Upper Saddle River, NJ

Dedication

This book is dedicated to the memory of my Mum, who remains my inspiration and will be forever in my heart and soul.

First published in the United States and Canada in 2004 by

CRE**A**TIVE
ARTS & CRAFTS™

An imprint of Creative Homeowner®
Upper Saddle River, NJ
Creative Homeowner® is a registered trademark of Federal Marketing Corp.

Current printing (last digit) 10 9 8 7 6 5 4 3 2 1
Library of Congress card number: 2004101634
ISBN: 1-58011-230-7

Senior Editor: Clare Sayer
Production: Hazel Kirkman
Design: AG&G Books Glyn Bridgewater
Photographer: Shona Wood
Editorial Direction: Rosemary Wilkinson

Printed and bound in Malaysia

Disclaimer

The author and publisher have made every effort to ensure that all instructions given in this book are safe and accurate, but they cannot accept liability for any resulting injuries or loss or damage to either property or person, whether direct or consequential and howsoever arising.

Acknowledgments

I would like to thank the following people for their contributions to this book: My team at NCW for their unfailing support: Clive, Debbie and Derrie, Lynne and Rodney, Arthur, Grace and Fern. Debbie and Ian for the provision of MDF blanks. Karl for his help and support base coating.

My editor Clare for her patience, understanding, and guidance, and Shona for her superb photography.

I would like to thank my sister Zoe; only she knows how much I rely on her. The phrase "sisters by birth, friends by choice" must simply have been written for her. There are no words that truly express how much she means to me. But most of all, my most ardent fan and supporter my Dad simply for being there.

And lastly this book is for everyone who shares the love of painting.

CREATIVE HOMEOWNER

A division of Federal Marketing Corp.
24 Park Way
Upper Saddle River, NJ 07458
www.creativehomeowner.com

Contents

Introduction *6*   Materials and equipment *8*   Preparation *12*   Techniques *13*

Projects

Lace tissue box *16*

Kitchen-utensil holder *20*

Neoclassical wall cabinet *24*

Primrose cachepot *28*

Floral pegged rack *32*

Rooster message board *36*

Bumble bee jewelry box *40*

Painted herb pots *44*

Plum-and-plum-leaf tray *48*

Bluebell lamp and shade *52*

Kitchen shelf with acorns *56*

Cabinet with lilies *60*

Ribbon-and-bow fire screen *64*

Morning-glory corner table *68*

Poppy-painted folding screen *72*

Templates *76*   Suppliers *78*   Index *80*

 Introduction

Welcome to the world of decorative painting. Have you ever admired a piece of painted furniture or stopped to study a beautiful painting and wondered how you could re-create something like it?

I have been painting for 15 years and the fascination has never worn off. When I open a new bottle of paint, I am like a child at Christmas, excited to see if the color is just the one I need to complete my picture. My mind is always racing with ideas, colors and images. I always carry a camera with me so that I can capture some of the lovely things round me: sunflowers turning to face the sun; dancing bluebells, bright and fresh from the earth; a field of fierce red poppies; or lilies with a sprinkling of morning dew. All of them are perfect inspirations for designs.

In this book, I have painted fresh and simple designs with easy step-by-step instructions. Most of the projects can be done by someone who is completely new to decorative painting, while others are a little more challenging. However, as you work your way through the book, you will progress and hopefully pick up some useful tips along the way. My aim is to remove some of the mystique surrounding decorative painting and to open up a whole new world of wonder.

When I first began painting, I just concentrated on creating artistic backgrounds or faux finishes. I could never get the courage to actually create a design on the surface. It has only been in the last few years that I have gained the confidence to develop my painting skills. I want to encourage you to paint because there is nothing stopping you. The first time a friend, family member, or colleague encourages you or praises your work, you will have crossed the boundaries into artistry and your creative world will never be the same again.

Perhaps I should finally confess that painting has changed my life I'm totally hooked. I find it relaxing, exciting, and completely absorbing. I hope that some of my enthusiasm rubs off a little. Now lets get painting!

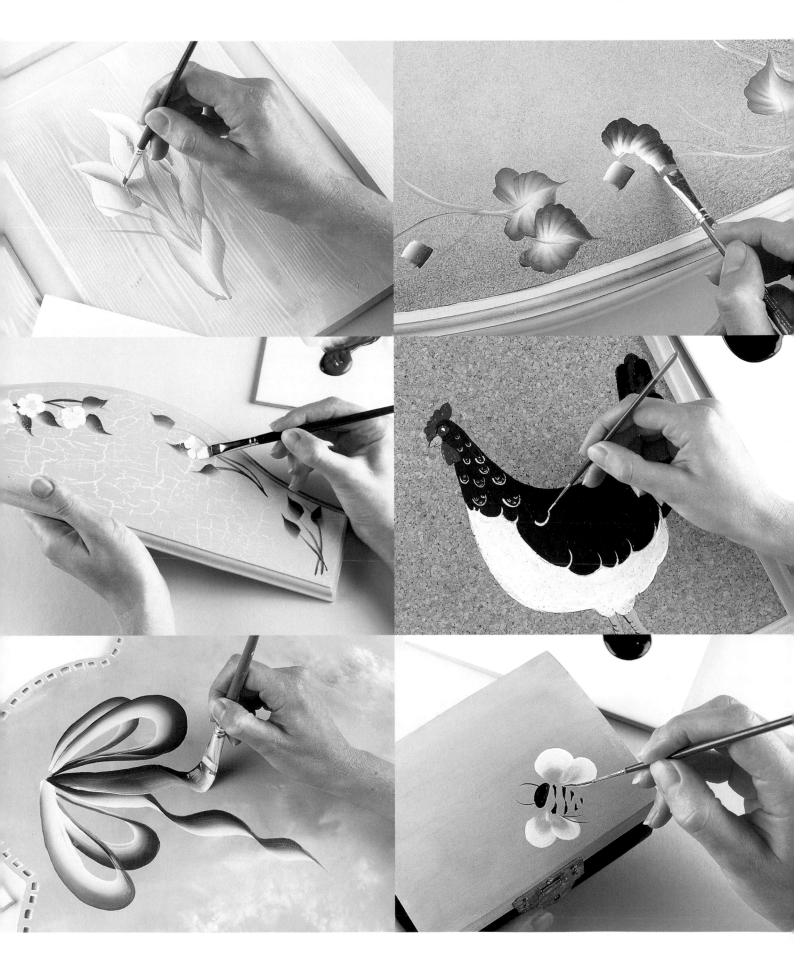

Materials and equipment

To get started, you will need some basic materials and equipment. However, much of the equipment you will need can be found around the home, so there is no need to rush out and spend a lot of money. Brushes and paints are obviously essential, but there are other things that will make your decorative painting easier.

Brushes

Artist's brushes can vary enormously in terms of shape, size, and price. Some are relatively good value while others are a substantial investment. There are several things to look for when buying brushes.

A brush is made up of a handle and bristles that are held together by a metal part called a ferrule. A good brush should have bristles that stay close together and spring back freely when pressed into the palm of your hand. A flat brush has a sharp chisel edge. The best way to test a chisel edge is to dip the brush in clean water and run the bristles from ferrule to tip through your fingers. The edge should stay sharp with the bristles together. Round and liner brushes should form fine points.

Brush bristle lengths can vary enormously. The general rule is that the longer the brush bristles the more flexible the brush, longer bristles hold more paint too. In comparison, shorter bristles are better for detail strokes.

The lengths of brush handles also vary considerably. For most decorative painting, you must hold the brush close to the ferrule. Good-quality brushes have the bristles that are glued and clamped into the ferrule. If the ferrule is loose, the bristles are more likely to shed onto your work; water can also make its way into the brush via a loose ferrule. This will damage your brushes.

Try not to get confused by the enormous number of different bristles. There are generally two main types: synthetic and natural. Synthetic brushes are much easier to use for the beginner and produce good results. They are also hard-wearing and reasonably priced. It is worth spending some time holding and becoming acquainted with your brushes, because your choice of brush can greatly affect your painting. The projects in this book only use a small selection of brushes.

Flat brushes have a flat metal ferrule and end in a sharp chisel edge. You can paint on the flat side to fill in areas or use the chisel edge for a fine line.

Round brushes end in a sharp point and come in many sizes. They are ideal for making petals and leaves.

Liner brushes are long and thin and tapered to a fine point. They are used for creating stems, stalks, tendrils, and curlicues.

Filbert brushes are similar to flat brushes, but they have rounded edges. They are good for applying a base coat and creating leaves.

Flogger brushes are made of very long natural hair and appear floppy and unsupported. They are used to "slap" a glazed surface to give it an aged appearance.

Stippling brushes are usually square; the bristles are long, stiff, and often made of hog hair. Stippling brushes take a lot of pressure so they need to be durable. The purpose of the brush is to stipple wet paint and create a textured effect on a flat surface. It is almost impossible to stipple on a rounded surface. To use it, hold the stippling brush in the palm of your hand and firmly tap a wet painted surface with the full force of the bristles to "texture" the paint. Some stippling brushes come with a long handle for ease of use. Personally I prefer to grab the brush firmly with the palm of my hand.

Looking after your brushes

If you look after your brushes they should last for a long time. Follow these simple rules and you will soon get into the habit of cleaning and storing them correctly:

Dos and Don'ts

- Never leave your brushes in water overnight. They will become waterlogged.
- Clean your brushes with the appropriate solvents. Use water if the paint or glaze is water-based (latex or acrylic, generally). Use turpentine or mineral spirits after using an alkyd-based paint or glaze.
- Clean your brushes after use. If paint is left to harden, the bristles will open and they will be ruined.
- Never scrub brushes to clean them; always draw the bristles inside a large pail or cardboard box.
- Never use your best sable brush for applying a base coat. I always save

my old brushes. They come in handy for the job. But a flat nylon brush works the best.

- Treat your brushes now and again to a little shampoo. Remember they have natural hair and will appreciate it.
- Never prop up wet brushes. Lay them flat to dry, and then store them.
- Use a bar of soap to clean your brushes. Do not scrub the bristles, just stroke them. Then work the soap into the bristles using your fingers. Or use dishwasing liquid.

Acrylic paints

There is a huge range of paints available now but water-based acrylic paints are the most widely used in decorative painting. They are far more versatile than their alkyd-based counterparts. Acrylics dry quickly, which makes them ideal for the busy decorative painter who wants to build layers of color without having to wait days for the project to dry. You can use water-based acrylics to mimic alkyd paints by adding various mediums, or thin them down and use them in a way similar to watercolors.

All colors of acrylic paint are made up of a select number of pure pigments. These pigments are made up from the three primary colors: red, yellow, and blue. The pure pigments are the same across all brands. Choosing your brand and color can be one of the most daunting things about beginning painting. A good-quality acrylic is smooth and creamy and heavily pigmented. Avoid paints that sound watery when shaken—you will find

that the paint has no real color or substance. Aim for middle of the range in price and pure pigments. Take one bottle home and try it out to see if you like that particular brand.

A manufacturer takes two or more pure pigments and mixes them to varying degrees to create the whole spectrum of colors.

Even with the variety of pre-mixed paints available, you may still want to mix your own colors. Color mixing can be daunting for the newcomer to decorative painting but it can also be

lots of fun. Remember that wet paint looks considerably different than dry paint. As it dries paint looses a little of the reflectiveness that comes with the moisture. Depending upon the depth of color, paint can lighten or darken and give an altogether a different result.

(The paint colors recommended for the projects in this book are from Plaid Paints' Folk Art acrylics palette. Comparable colors are made by other manufacturers. See Suppliers, page 78.)

Other useful equipment

Tracing paper and transfer paper

They are essential for tracing designs and transferring them onto your surface. Lay the tracing paper over the design and use a sharp pencil or fine stylus to go over the lines. Transfer paper acts in the same way as carbon paper but, unlike carbon paper, it won't leave a residue. It is available in light and dark colors. Position the transfer paper between the surface and the traced design and use a little masking tape to secure it. Go over the traced lines with a pencil.

Painting palette

There are many palettes on the market, but a plain ceramic tile makes a good palette for loading paint. A good-quality palette should have sufficient space for at least 12 colors and a large blending area. Most palettes are made of durable plastic, which is easy to wash.

Brush basin

A brush basin is a useful item in decorative painting, although a jam jar also works well. A brush basin will have two or three compartments and is designed to hold a number of brushes.

Acetate sheets

These are useful for practicing brush strokes and blending and are widely available from craft stores. Simply wipe the sheet clean and start again.

Acrylic sealant and varnish

Most surface preparation requires the use of a good water-based sealant or varnish, especially when painting onto medium-density fiberboard (MDF) or new wood. Use a sealant to prepare a surface, and a varnish to protect the finish. Wait at least 24 hours after completing the project before varnishing. There are several options when it comes to choosing a sealant. You can use watered-down polyvinyl adhesive (PVA): one part PVA to four parts water. Because it is flexible, it does a good job. When choosing a sealant or varnish always make sure that the contents are water-based and non-yellowing.

It is always best to apply several thin coats and build up the protection gradually, rather than applying one thick coat. The only time I apply a thick coat of varnish is if I want a heavy-gloss finish on a completely flat project. Thicker layers of varnish give the appearance of a mirrored surface. When applying varnish or sealant, do not over brush, or you will work bubbles into the surface. Don't be tempted to go back over an area several minutes after you have applied the varnish because it will have already started to dry and you will mar the smooth finish.

Tack cloth

Tack cloths are used to remove dust, grease, and debris from wood and MDF surfaces. You can also use a clean cotton or linen cloth.

Steel wool

Steel wool is produced using high-quality steel to create a crumble- and dust-resistant wool, which is virtually oil-free and will not leave any rogue strands. Most steel wool is packed in rolls so you can cut convenient sized strips with scissors. There are various grades of steel wool for different jobs. If you are unsure of which to use, go for a fine grade. Steel wool is used to prepare old or painted wood surfaces by gently rubbing over the surface.

Scumble or sponging glaze

Scumble glaze is a milky white liquid that dries to a transparent finish. It provides you with increased "open time." This means that your mixture will stay wet longer so that you can move the paint around on your surface. Many paint effects, such as wood graining, rag rolling, and stippling are achieved using sponging glaze. You can color sponging glaze using acrylic paints. It remains workable for many minutes, but once it begins to dry you cannot go back over it because it will drag the paint. Remember that a glaze can take up to 24 hours to cure completely.

Fine-grade sandpaper

Preparing items before painting is an essential part of the process. Sanding prepares a surface to bond with paint. Always wear a mask when sanding.

Natural sponge

Natural sponges are used to create sponged effects, often over a large area. Synthetic sponges do not work as well as natural ones because they do not have the texture to create a mottled look.

Wood-graining tool

This useful piece of equipment is used to create the effect of wood graining on MDF or other surfaces.

Gold leaf

Imitation gold-leaf sheets are used, along with special sizing, to create a gilded effect.

Paper towels and rags

These are always good to have to hand in case of spills.

Preparation

Choosing the surfaces

There are many materials available to the decorative painter. You may already have something at home that you could paint. Medium Density Fiberboard (MDF) is a wood-based composite material that uses wood fibers, rather than particles or veneers, to produce board or sheet products. MDF is available at home-improvement centers in large or pre-cut sheets. One of its advantages is that it absorbs far less surface moisture than timber, so applying a base coat is quick and easy. It will also retain its original shape and is fire- and heat-resistant. Wood glues, nails, and staples can all be used to securely hold surfaces together. Just don't let it stay damp for long periods—it will swell. You may want to experiment and create your own blanks; however, there are many companies that supply MDF pieces, ready for painting.

Wood is an ideal surface for painting, and it does not need to be new wood. Painted wood can be transformed by simply removing the layers of old paint to reveal the raw wood. You can paint directly onto a painted surface, but you should sand it and use a sealant.

Terra cotta is often used for decorative painting because its surface is smooth and porous. If you seal the surface first you will be able to wipe off any mistakes easily. When painting terra cotta for outside use, an outdoor sealer must also be applied after you have painted the design. When choosing terra cotta surfaces, look for those with a clean surface area. Any corrosion or permanent staining means the paint will flake and often crack.

Preparing MDF and plywood

Always prepare your surface before painting your design.

1 First, remove any dust and dirt with a tack cloth. Rub lightly over the surface with a fine-grade sandpaper. Wipe it once again with a tack cloth to remove the sawdust.

2 Next, using a clean flat brush, apply a thin coat of water-based sealant. (Use store-bought sealant or mix 1 part PVA watered down with 4 parts water.) Apply the sealant quickly at this stage because the MDF is absorbent and the sealant will soak quickly into your surface.

3 Using a clean flat brush, apply a thin base coat. Try not to go over the same area too many times, to keep the surface smooth. Allow it to dry for at least 30 minutes. For the best results, apply two or three thin coats of base color, and sand the surface after each coat is dry.

Preparing old wood

Before preparing any old or unsealed wood surfaces, check whether the wood you are painting has been treated with an oil-based product. If so, lightly sand the wood, go over it with a cloth, and apply a coat of sealant.

Preparing painted wood

1 Using a rough-grade sandpaper, sand the wood down to the grain. You can use an electric sander for this. Always exercise caution when operating machinery. Do not exert too much pressure on the wood. Once most of the dirt has been removed, wipe over the surface with soapy water. Allow it to dry.

2 If you feel the wood is not quite smooth enough, take a fine-grade sandpaper and gently sand over it once again. Use the palm of your hand to judge the smoothness of surface. Once again, wipe the wood with a tack cloth.

3 Using a flat brush, apply a coat of water-based sealant. Allow it to dry.

Preparing terra cotta

Terra cotta is a very porous surface that will absorb a lot of moisture. Leave the terra cotta surface to stand in a dry place for at least two days before painting.

1 Make sure the surface is completely dry. Wipe the surface with a clean dry cloth. Using a flat brush, apply a thin coat of sealant over the whole surface area. Allow it to dry.

2 If a base coat is required, apply it with a clean, flat brush.

Techniques

Now that you have a basic knowledge of the paints and equipment, as well as an understanding of the surfaces, it's time to start painting! First, make sure that you are sitting comfortably and that you have enough room—there is nothing worse than being cramped. Make sure your arms can hang freely and are not resting on the table. Elbows should also be off the table. You should paint from the shoulder, which means that you will be using your entire arm, shoulder, and little finger together in all stroke work.

Loading a flat brush

Correct brush control and loading will make the difference between good and great results. Pour out a puddle of each color onto your palette, making sure you have left enough space for blending. Draw the brush back and forth through the puddle of paint, working slowly and carefully. A thoroughly loaded brush will have paint loaded through the bristles. Stroke the brush back and forth through the edge of the paint. Never push the brush through the paint; draw it toward you in a fluid motion.

The brush should be loaded with paint two-thirds of the way up the bristles. Make sure that there are no blobs clinging to the bristles. The chisel edge of the brush should stay tight and sharp. If it begins to open up this means that the paint has worked too far into the brush and is pushing the bristles apart. If you need to practice a few times, start again by drawing the brush through a clean rag to remove most of the paint. For most brush work, the brush should be held perpendicular to the surface you are painting. This gives you greater control over the brush.

Side-loading

1 A side-loaded brushstroke has a solid color running through the stroke fading to a different color on one side. There should be no distinctive line where the color changes. Start by loading a single color onto a flat brush and work it into the bristles. Now dip one corner of the brush into a second color.

Double-loading

1 Dip the bristles of the brush into one color, making sure that the front and back of the brush are covered. Now lay the opposite side of the brush into the second color.

2 The brush should have two triangles of color. Work the paint into the brush by stroking back and forth across your palette. Re-load the brush as before and work the paint into the brush.

2 Work this back and forth to blend the color, reloading the second color as necessary.

Tipping

This is mostly done with a round brush to create a highlight.
1 Take a fully loaded round brush, and dip the tip into a second color.

2 Tap off a little of the excess paint onto a tile. Blend the second color slightly into the brush.

Loading a round brush

A round brush is loaded in a similar way to the flat brush. Load paint two-thirds of the way up the bristles. Roll it in your fingers through the paint. This will gather paint on the brush. Rolling keeps the shape of the brush perfectly.

Line stroke

This is used for painting straight lines. Use a well-loaded flat brush. Stand the brush on the flat edge and pull it toward you while painting a thin line. Always use the flat of the brush.

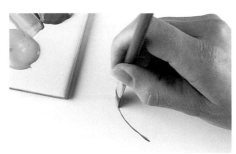

Flat-leaf stroke

Double-load a flat brush. Start on the chisel edge and press down while turning and sliding. Start to lift the brush back up onto the chisel edge to complete the stroke.

Leaf stroke

1 Double-load a flat brush. Place the brush on the chisel edge, and start the stroke by pushing the brush

down, then wiggle it to create a ruffle, sliding back to the chisel edge.
2 Complete the leaf with either a flat stroke or another wiggly stroke drawn close under the first leaf.

"C" stroke

"C" strokes are used for painting fruit such as plums, apples, or grapes, as well as the petals of certain flowers.
1 Double-load a flat brush. Apply the chisel edge of the brush to the surface, and slide one side a short distance, making a slight arc.

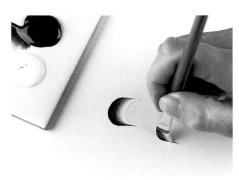

2 Continue into a curve, and press down slightly so that you are using the whole width of the brush. As you

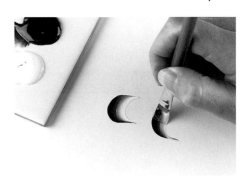

complete the curve, ease the pressure on the brush and bring it back onto the chisel edge, parallel with where you started. This may take some practice, as it needs to be done in one smooth motion with a fully loaded brush.

Flower-petal stroke

1 Double-load a flat brush. With the brush on the chisel edge, push, turn and slide in a slight arc to the top center of the flower. Pull the brush in slightly and back to the chisel edge. Complete the petal by pushing, turning, and sliding back down to the bottom of the petal.

2 Create a flower by positioning petals together in a circle (most flowers have five petals). A variation is to wiggle the brush on the way up and on the way back down to create a more defined finish.

Swirls and tendrils

These are best painted using a script-liner brush or rigger. Mix an inky puddle by using a little water to thin down the paint.
1 Load the brush by splaying the bristles of the brush in the paint before rolling the brush through the

paint. This will keep the brush loaded with enough paint.

2 With your little finger stuck out to help you keep you hand steady, swirl the brush round in circles back and forth and in different directions. Your arm must be loose for the stroke to appear natural.

Artist's tips

Color mixing If you mix a color specifically for any project, whether it is for the base coat or design, always make sure to mix enough and put the leftovers in a old jar or clean bottle. It is a good idea to make a note of what colors you have used in case you ever need to touch up or want to make a duplicate of a finished item.

Sanding wood surfaces When sanding down any wood surface, whether you are using sandpaper or an electric sander, always sand in the direction of the grain. If you sand against the grain, you will score the surface of the wood and cause damage.

Paint stripping When removing paint, I try to avoid using turpentine or mineral spirit, which can be damaging to the wood. However, on occasion it is necessary. If you must use these solvents, wear suitable protection and work in a well-ventilated area.

Varnishing Varnish will remain tacky for a long time, far longer that acrylic products. Always make sure any project is left to dry in a clean well-ventilated area away from dust and hairs. Never sand or apply further coats of varnish until the most recent one is completely dry. When working with spray sealers, always work in a well-ventilated area or outside and wear the correct protection.

Lace tissue box

This pretty pink tissue box with its lacy design is a delight to look at and paint. The pattern is delicate yet simple enough for an absolute beginner to achieve an exceptionally professional result.

Although at first glance the design appears intricate, this light and airy look is easy to achieve.

You will need

Materials

- MDF tissue box
- Acrylic paint in the following colors: pale pink, white
- Tracing paper
- Transfer paper
- Masking tape
- Water-based varnish

Tools

- Fine sandpaper
- Tack cloth
- Tile or palette
- 1 in. flat brush
- Natural sponge
- Pencil or stylus
- ½-in. flat brush
- No. 1 liner brush

1 Prepare the surface for painting by sanding lightly and going over with a tack cloth. Using the 1-inch flat brush, apply a base coat to the tissue box using pale pink acrylic paint.

2 Mix equal parts of white acrylic paint and water. Using a damp natural sponge, go over the tissue box by dabbing the surface quickly and evenly with paint. The water in the paint will evaporate and dry clear, leaving a lacy translucent effect. Leave it to dry thoroughly.

★☆☆ **Skill level**   🕐 **2¹/₂ hours**   **Techniques:** *Line stroke p. 14*

3 Trace the design on page 76 onto tracing paper. Transfer the design onto the tissue box by placing the transfer paper between the tracing paper and the project. Make sure to line the pattern to the edge of the tissue box side, and hold it in place with masking tape. Use a pencil or stylus to go over the traced lines. Remove the paper and tape before painting the project.

4 Side-load a ½-inch flat brush with white acrylic paint and water. Paint from the edge to the scallop lines. Then paint in the scallops. Leave to dry.

5 Using the liner brush, trace in any fine lines on the pattern. Using the handle end of the brush, pick up some white paint and add the dots to the design. Remember to re-load the end of the brush to create dots of a uniform size. Leave it to dry.

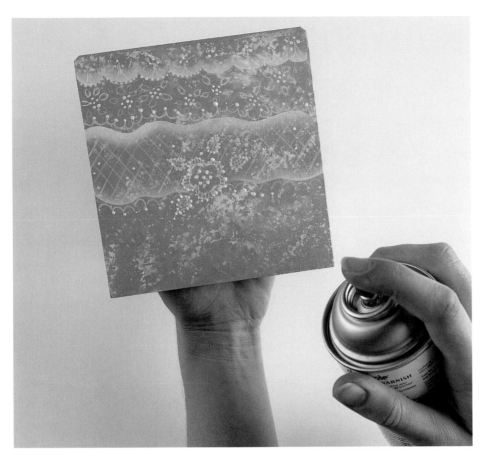

6 Once the project is completely dry, seal it with a water-based varnish. Use two coats if necessary.

Helpful hint

When using a spray varnish, always hold the spray can at least 3 inches away from the surface for an even finish.

Variation

Memory box

This design works well on many different surfaces including papier-mache. Once you have mastered the technique of dotting, try your hand at this lovely round box. It would make a ideal gift for storing precious memories. Line the box with fabric for an elegant finish.

Kitchen-utensil holder

Ferns are unbelievably easy to paint. Beginners and advanced painters alike can produce equally professional results, so don't limit them to just this project. By varying the size and shades of green, you can make ferns the perfect embellishment for other surfaces.

To make cleaning this utensil holder easier, use a non-yellowing, water-based polyurethane varnish to seal the project.

You will need

Materials
- Utensil holder
- Acrylic paints in the following colors: light orange, white, Hauser green dark, bayberry
- Sponging glaze
- Water-based varnish

Tools
- Fine sandpaper
- Tack cloth
- Tile or palette
- 1-in. flat brush
- Flogger brush
- ½-in. flat brush

1 Prepare the surface for painting by sanding lightly and going over with a tack cloth. Using the 1-inch flat brush, apply a base coat of light orange acrylic paint. Apply two coats if necessary. Leave to dry.

2 Mix equal parts of white acrylic paint and sponging glaze. Using the same brush, paint one side at a time with the colored glaze.

3 While the glaze is still wet, take the flogger brush and drag the full length of the bristles down the surface of the utensil holder in one stroke. Overlap the strokes until the whole area is covered. Complete the other sides in the same way.

Helpful hint
If you make a mistake when you are using the flogger brush, then simply paint over it again with glaze. Always make sure the glaze is completely dry before painting the design over the top.

4 Double-load a ½-inch flat brush with Hauser green dark and bayberry. Paint the stems by sliding the brush on the chisel edge, making sure the handle is upright. Lead with the bayberry. To paint the fronds of the fern, slide the double-loaded brush on the chisel edge working from the stem outwards.

5 To fill in the leaves of the fern, double-load the ½-inch flat brush with Hauser green dark and bayberry. Start at the top of each frond and work down to the bottom. Vary the distance between the leaves.

6 Once the project is completely dry, apply two protective coats of varnish. Lightly sand between coats, if necessary.

Variation

Framed painting

Often the simplest of paintings looks stunning when placed inside a frame. Why not vary this idea and produce your own limited-edition "paintings." Number each one in the corner with a pencil to add authenticity.

Neoclassical wall cabinet

Neoclassical style offers something a little more refined. With striking motifs as its signature elements, the stunning design on this wall cabinet epitomizes all things elegant and timeless. The motif on the top of the cabinet is repeated inside.

When transferring the design, don't worry about the detail because this will be covered over with the base coat. To reposition your pattern accurately, cut out the entire shape and reposition it as a template before marking in the detail once again.

You will need

Materials
- Wall cabinet
- Acrylic paint in the following colors: white, mink, lavender
- Tracing paper
- Transfer paper
- Masking tape
- Transparent medium
- Water-based varnish

Tools
- Fine sandpaper
- Tack cloth
- Tile or palette
- 1-in. flat brush
- Pencil or stylus
- ½-in. flat brush
- Round brush
- No. 1 liner brush

1 Prepare the surface for painting. Apply a base coat to the inside and exposed edges of the cabinet using white acrylic paint. Paint the top and outer sides in the mink color. Leave it to dry.

Helpful hint
When using a light-color base coat, always apply two coats for a good even coverage. Apply the base coat with a clean flat brush. The size of brush should be determined by the size of the area that needs paint.

★☆☆ **Skill level** 🕐 **3 hours** **Techniques:** *Side-loading p. 13*

2 Trace the design on page 77 onto tracing paper and re-size it to fit your project. Use a photocopier, if necessary. Position the transfer paper between the tracing paper and project, making sure to line the pattern to the top edge of the cabinet. Hold it in place with masking tape and use a pencil or stylus to trace the design.

3 To paint the design on the top of the cabinet, apply a base coat within the outline of the design using white paint and using a ½-inch flat brush. Leave it to dry thoroughly.

4 Double-load a ½-inch flat brush with lavender paint and transparent medium. Paint the top of the cabinet, working around the design and to the edges. Trace the outline to shade the whole design.

5 Paint in the detail by loading a round brush with lavender and reloading when necessary. Use the original template as a reference for where to put the detail.

6 Finish the design by adding some white highlights using the liner brush.

7 Repeat the design inside the cabinet. There is no need to apply a white base coat this time. Apply a coat of varnish once the project is dry.

Helpful hint

A three-dimensional look is created on this project using only two paint colors. Take time on the shading. This will increase the perception of a raised design, making the overall effect far more striking.

Primrose cachepot

Summer is always here with this pretty yellow cachepot decorated with primroses. Primroses are a delight to look at and an even greater pleasure to paint. This project also features a marble effect made with smoke.

Finish the edges of the project
by painting them in gold.

You will need

Materials

- MDF cachepot
- Acrylic paint in the following colors: sunflower, white, orange, bayberry, Hauser green dark, gold
- Water-based varnish

Tools

- Fine sandpaper
- Tack cloth
- Tile or palette
- 1-in. flat brush
- Candle
- Plastic-handled scissors
- ½-in. flat brush
- Liner brush

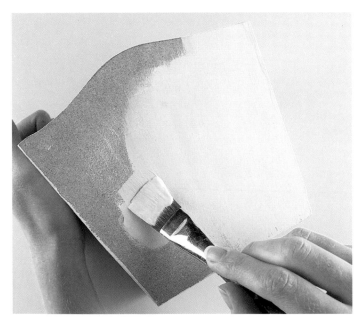

1 Prepare the surface for painting. Apply a base coat in sunflower to all the sides. Leave it to dry. Use two coats, if necessary, for a professional finish. Don't forget to paint underneath and inside of the cachepot.

2 To create a smoke-marble effect, hold the metal blades of a pair of scissors over a candle flame. Black smoke will start to rise from the flame. Move the cachepot gently over the smoke. Do not linger over the flame or the effect will be too dark. Leave it for at least 30 minutes before sealing the surface with a water-based varnish. Leave it to dry.

★☆☆ **Skill level**   ⏱ **3 hours**   **Techniques:** *Wiggly leaf p. 14, Flower petal p. 15*

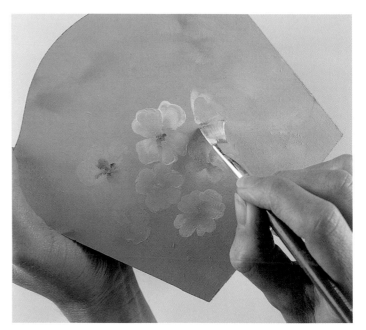

3 To paint the design, load a ½-inch brush with white paint, then side-load opposite sides with orange and sunflower paint. Work the paint through the brush by stroking back and forth on the tile. You can paint the design freehand or, if you prefer, transfer the design on page 76.

4 Each flower has five petals. For the first petal, with the orange in the center of the flower, pivot the chisel edge of the brush and turn the outer edge while pushing down. Lift back to the chisel edge for the top of the flower and complete the second half of the petal in the same way. Repeat for the other petals.

5 To create the center of the flower, dip the liner brush in orange and dot the center of the flower.

Helpful hint

When painting delicate strokes or fine detail, use your little finger to steady your hand.

6 To paint the flower stems, double-load the ½-inch flat brush with bayberry and Hauser green dark paints. Slide the brush along the chisel edge. To paint the leaves, double-load the ½-inch flat brush with Hauser green dark and bayberry. Start at the base of the leaf on the chisel edge of the brush, and use the Hauser green dark for the outside of the leaf. Apply pressure and wiggle the brush up and down while sliding it along the length of the leaf. Pivot the brush as you turn at top of the leaf to come down the other side. If necessary, re-load the brush between each side of the leaf stroke.

Variation

Smoke-marbled roses

This variation combines the traditional look of roses with classic smoke marbling. Smoke marbling makes a great background finish for any of the projects in this book. The roses are created using two "C" strokes.

Floral pegged rack

This fresh and zesty crackle-glazed pegged rack certainly jumps out at you. This project is perfect for a beginner because the design is so simple.

It is easier to paint the project without the coat hooks attached. When the project is complete, you can re-attach them.

You will need

Materials

- Coat-hook rack
- Acrylic paints in the following colors: turquoise, bright green, Hauser green dark, sunflower, white
- Crackle glaze
- Water-based varnish

Tools

- Fine sandpaper
- Tack cloth
- Tile or palette
- 1-in. flat brush
- ½-in. flat brush
- No. 1 liner brush

1 Prepare the surface for painting by sanding it lightly and going over it with a tack cloth. Using the 1-inch flat brush, apply a base coat in turquoise. Leave it to dry.

2 Apply a coat of crackle glaze with a good firm hand. Do not overbrush. Leave it to dry.

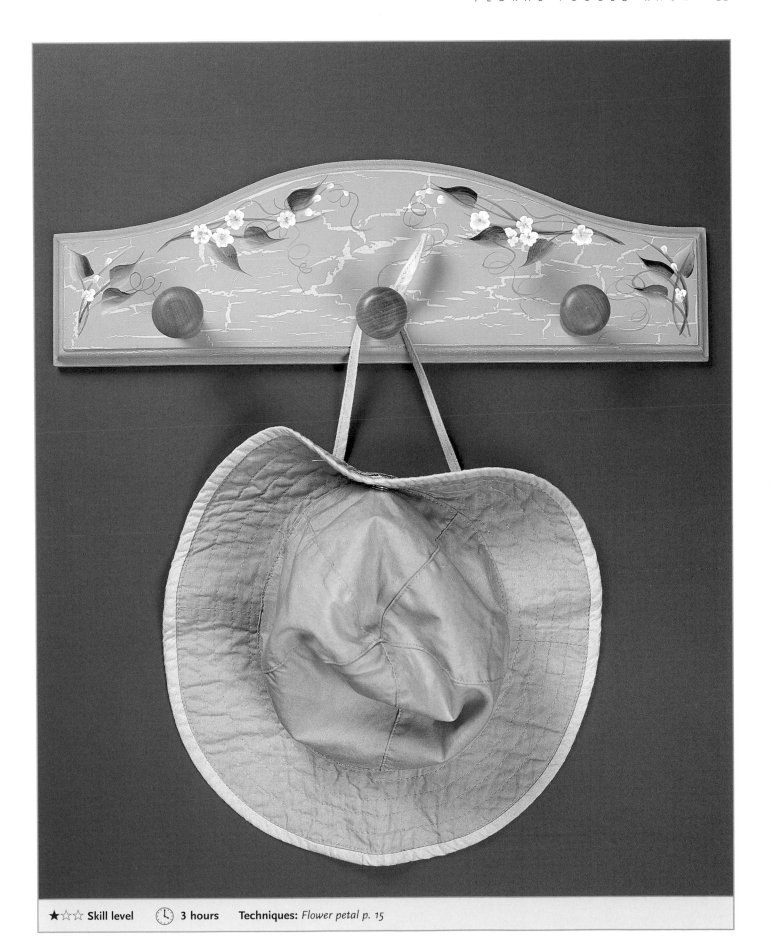

★☆☆ **Skill level**   🕐 **3 hours**   **Techniques:** *Flower petal p. 15*

3 Add a little water to the bright green paint. Without overlapping the brush strokes, apply an even coat in this color. As this top coat dries, cracks will begin to appear. Leave it to dry thoroughly.

4 The direction of the stems determines the position of the design. Double-load the ½-inch flat brush with Hauser green dark and sunflower paint and apply a line stroke by sliding the brush on the chisel edge, keeping the handle upright and the sunflower paint away from you.

5 Next paint the flat leaves using the ½-inch flat brush double-loaded with Hauser green dark and sunflower paints. With the brush on the chisel edge, push down, pivot the brush to turn the top color, and gently release the pressure while sliding back up onto the chisel to complete the leaf. Re-load and repeat for each leaf.

6 To paint the flowers, double-load a ½-inch flat brush with white and sunflower paints. Re-load the brush for each petal. With the brush on the chisel edge, push, turn, and slide in an arc to the top center of the flower. Pull the brush in slightly and bring it back to the chisel edge. Complete the flower by pushing, turning, and sliding the brush back down to the bottom of the petal. Complete each flower this way. For the center of the flower, dip the end of the handle in Hauser green dark paint and dot the center.

7 To paint the tendrils, mix Hauser green dark and water to the consistency of ink and then load the liner brush. Hold the brush above the ferrule; extend your little finger to improve balance; and paint loops overlapping each other back and forth in opposite directions. Leave the project to dry completely before applying a coat of varnish.

Helpful hint

When applying crackle glaze, do not make a lot of passes with the brush. A thicker coat of crackle will produce thicker cracks in the top coat of paint.

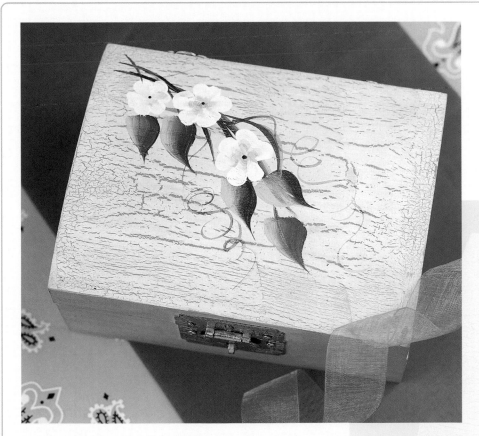

Variation

Victorian jewelry box

Even though the flowers are the same, more subtle colors have been used in this variation and the overall look is far more subdued and elegant. To create a softer effect, apply a thinner coat of crackle glaze. This will create smaller, less defined cracks in the paint.

Rooster message board

This project is simplicity itself: fun, quick, and really easy. It's a great gift for a friend, or perfect for the kitchen wall. The bright and breezy rooster design shows that decorative painting is not just about painting flowers.

Cork is a great surface for paint .It's simple, smooth, and absorbent. Once the design has been transferred, the enjoyment is in the painting.

You will need

Materials
- Corkboard
- Tracing paper
- Acrylic paint in the following colors: black, white, red, yellow ochre, green
- Masking tape (optional)

Tools
- Pencil
- Stylus
- Tile or palette
- Small round brush
- No. 1 liner brush
- ½-in. flat brush

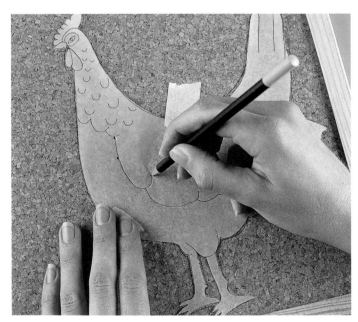

1 Trace the design on page 76 and resize as necessary. Cut out the pattern and, using it as an outline, transfer the design onto the corkboard using a pencil. For the detail, pierce small holes through the pattern using a stylus. Remove the pattern and join the dots with a pencil.

2 Using the photograph to identify the positions of each of the colors, start by applying the base coat to the rooster using a small round brush loaded with black paint. Leave it to dry.

3 Again, using the photograph as a guide, apply a white base coat. Leave it to dry. Continue to paint the rooster by adding the red detail of the head using a small round brush. Next apply a base coat in yellow ochre on to the beak and legs using the same round brush. Clean the brush before using a new color.

Helpful hint
Reduce or enlarge the design on a photocopier to fit the surface of the project, then cut out the outline.

4 Load the liner brush with black and add the detail to the chicken feet. Clean the brush and load with white. Add the feather details to the chicken.

5 To paint the grass, double-load a ½-inch flat brush with green and yellow ochre paint. Slide the brush along the chisel edge from the center of each group of grass, leading with the yellow ochre color.

6 Paint the frame red using the ½-inch flat brush. Masking off the cork, if necessary. Alternatively dilute the paint with water making a 50:50 solution for a washed-wood effect.

Variation

Kitchen clock

The rooster looks fun and quirky on this kitchen clock. To transfer the design onto the clock, photocopy and cut out the pattern. Then use it as an outline to trace onto the clock surface. (If possible, remove the hands of the clock before transferring the design.) Try painting other kitchen items for a fun, fresh, and coordinated look.

Bumble bee jewelry box

Here's a completely different look for a jewelry box. It's very minimalistic, making it a perfect gift for someone who prefers simplicity. Bumble bees are a pleasure to paint, they make a great accent for a floral design.

'Inky black' refers to the consistency of the mix of paint and water. When loading a brush with inklike paint, splay the bristles out before rolling the brush though the paint to make sure the brush has sufficient paint to complete the stroke.

You will need

Materials
- Jewelry box
- Acrylic paint in the following colors: French blue, black, yellow ochre, white
- Transparent medium
- Gloss varnish

Tools
- Fine sandpaper
- Tack cloth
- Tile or palette
- 1-in. flat brush
- ½-in. flat brush
- Small round brush
- No. 1 liner brush

1 Prepare the surface for painting by sanding it lightly and going over it with a tack cloth. Load the 1-inch flat brush with French blue paint and apply a base coat to the lid of the jewelry box. Leave it to dry thoroughly.

2 Apply a black base coat to the bottom of the jewelry box. Leave it to dry thoroughly.

3 Load a ½-inch flat brush with yellow ochre paint for the body of the bumble bee. Make a large flat stroke starting on the chisel edge and, applying pressure, bring the brush back to finish at the center of the tail of the bumble bee.

4 For the wings, double-load a ½-inch flat brush with transparent medium and white paint. Starting on the chisel edge with the transparent medium next to the body, pivot the brush taking the white paint around the outer edge of each of the four wings.

5 For the head of the bee, load a small round brush with black paint and make an oval shape.

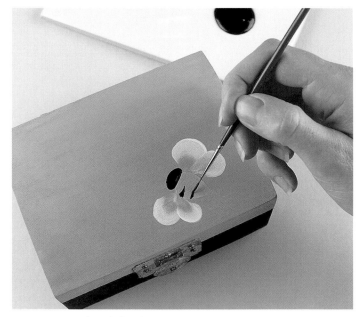

6 Next, load the liner brush with black paint and make a thin line for each of the body highlights.

7 Mix black paint with a little water until you have an inklike consistency. Load the liner brush by rolling it in the paint, and make the legs and antennae.

8 Load the liner brush with white paint and make the highlights on the eyes. When the project is completely dry, seal the base of the jewelry box with gloss varnish. Leave it to dry.

Variation

Bumble bee candles

These bold and striking colors lend themselves perfectly to candle painting. Wipe the surface of the candle with a paper towel before painting. This will give the paint a smoother finish and stop it from separating on the waxy surface.

Never leave a burning candle unattended.

Painted herb pots

These terra cotta pots are perfect for planting different herbs, and they look great grouped together on a kitchen windowsill.

Painted pots look decorative and let you bring your own herb garden into the kitchen.

You will need

Materials

- 3 terra cotta pots
- Water-based sealant
- Acrylic paint in the following colors: butter crunch, bayberry, cream, Hauser green dark, gray plum
- Water-based varnish

Tools

- Tile or palette
- 1-inch flat brush
- ½-inch flat brush
- No. 1 liner brush

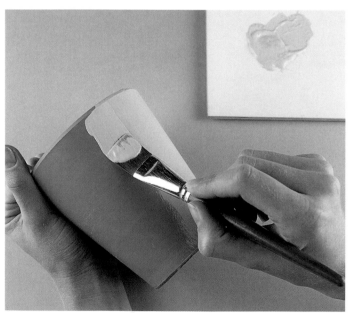

1 Prepare the terra cotta surfaces for painting. (See page 12.) Make sure you seal the inside and outside the pots. Using the 1-inch flat brush, apply a base coat to all of the pots using the butter crunch paint. Use two coats if necessary. Leave it to dry.

2 Using a ½-inch flat brush loaded with bayberry, paint a rectangle. Leave it to dry.

★☆☆ **Skill level** 🕐 **2½ hours** **Techniques:** *Line stroke p. 14*

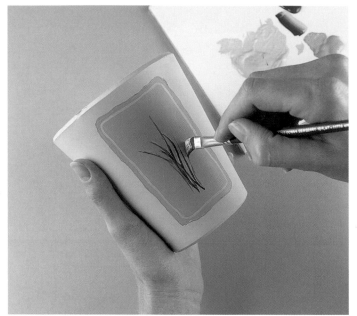

3 Using the liner brush loaded with cream paint, make a line just inside the painted rectangles on each pot. The line doesn't have to be perfectly straight or even. Support the brush by resting your little finger on the side of the pot.

4 For the chives, double-load a ½-inch flat brush with Hauser green dark and butter crunch paints. With the brush on the chisel edge, lead with the Hauser green dark paint and slide the brush the full length of each leaf. Make sure the chisel edge is sharp for each stroke.

5 For the thyme, double-load a ½-inch flat brush with Hauser green dark and gray plum paints. Lead with gray plum and paint the stems by keeping the brush handle straight. Next, with the gray plum towards the stem and the Hauser green dark on the outside, touch the chisel edge to the surface of the pot for each individual leaf. For longer leaves slide the brush very slightly towards the stem.

Helpful hint
It is much easier to hold the pot in your free hand when painting these designs.

6 For the mint, double-load a ½-inch flat brush with Hauser green dark and butter crunch paints. Make the stems, starting with the tops with Hauser green dark to the outside of each leaf. Wiggle the brush slightly from the base of each leaf to the tip. Repeat this for each leaf until the project is complete. When all of the terra cotta pots are dry, apply a protective coat of varnish. If the terra cotta is going outside, seal it with a durable outdoor varnish.

Variation

Lazy Susan herbs

Another variation on this design is to paint the herbs bunched together. Rich greens nestled together give the appearance of crisp fresh herbs. This project is a lazy Susan with the herbs under the glass. As with all items painted for the kitchen, make sure you protect the surface with a good quality varnish.

Plum-and-plum-leaf tray

The rich colors of summer fruits are a perfect complement to the sumptuous gilding effect that adorns this classical tray. Using basic brush-loading techniques, it is possible to paint plums that are shaded and highlighted using a few simple strokes. This creates the illusion that you have spent hours blending, when in fact, you have painted the plums in just a few minutes.

Vary the size of brushes to accommodate the size of fruit.

You will need

Materials

- MDF tray
- Acrylic paint in the following colors: barnyard red, white, night sky, berry wine, evergreen, sunflower, gold
- Masking tape
- Shellac
- Gold size
- Talcum powder
- Imitation gold leaf
- Sponging glaze
- Water-based varnish

Tools

- Fine sandpaper
- Tack cloth
- Tile or palette
- 1-in. flat brush
- Ruler
- Soft brush
- Plastic wrap
- ³/₄-in. flat brush
- ¹/₂-in. flat brush
- No. 1 liner brush

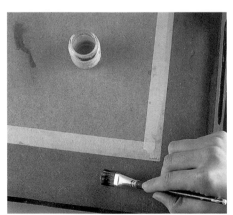

1 Prepare the surface for painting by sanding it lightly and going over it with a tack cloth. Using the 1-inch flat brush, apply a barnyard red base coat to the edges and outsides of the tray. Leave it to dry. Mask off a rectangle in the center of the tray using masking tape and a ruler. Seal the border and inner sides of the tray with shellac. Leave it to dry.

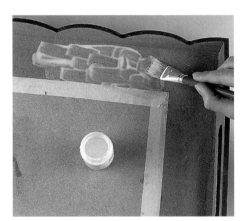

2 Apply an even coat of gold size to the shellacked area. Let it dry for 20 minutes. By that time the size should have lost its milky color and feel tacky. Remove the masking tape.

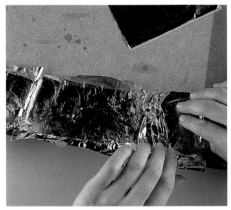

3 Coat your fingers with a little talcum powder to keep the gold leaf from sticking to you. Lay sheets of gold leaf over the sized area, pressing them down gently. Don't worry if they overlap.

★★☆ **Skill level**   🕐 **4 hours**   **Techniques:** *Flat leaf, "C" stroke p. 14, Flower petal p. 15*

4 Use a soft brush to remove any excess gold leaf and leave a smooth surface.

5 Once the gold leafing is complete, apply a base coat to the center panel using barnyard red paint. Go back over any areas that need more paint. Leave it to dry.

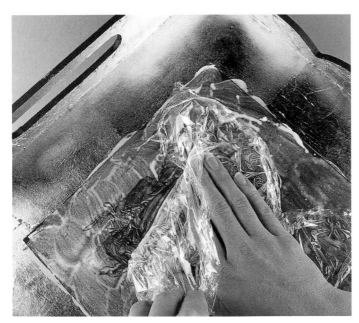

6 Mix equal parts of white paint and glaze and brush the mixture on to the center panel. While it is wet, lay plastic wrap over the top, crumpling it with your fingers. Press it down. Remove the plastic wrap, and leave the surface to dry. Trace the design on page 77 and transfer it onto the tray using template paper.

7 Double-load the ¾-inch brush with night sky and berry wine paints and then side-load white paint onto the edge with the berry wine. Paint a "C" stroke in the center with the berry wine. Next, slightly in from the top edge of the "C" stroke, paint an oval. Re-load the brush as necessary and repeat for all of the plums.

8 To paint the stems, double-load a ½-inch flat brush with evergreen and sunflower paints. Slide the brush along the chisel edge, away from each of the plums, in various directions to create the stems. Lead each stroke with the sunflower paint.

9 For the leaves, double-load the ½-inch flat brush with evergreen and sunflower paints. Place the brush on chisel edge and, pushing it down, turn and slide the brush while lifting it back to the chisel edge. Paint larger leaves using two strokes and keep the sunflower color in the center.

10 Each flower has five petals. Load the ½-inch flat brush with white paint; side-load with sunflower. With the sunflower paint in the center, pivot the chisel edge and turn the outer edge while wiggling the brush slightly. Repeat for the other petals. Dip the end of the handle in night sky paint and dot the flower centers.

11 Fill in any areas with small flat leaves using a ½-inch brush loaded with gold paint. Mix white paint and water until you have an ink consistency and load the liner brush by drawing it through the paint. Make overlapping loops. (Practice this first.) Once the project is dry, seal it with water-based varnish.

Bluebell lamp and shade

Fresh and simple, bluebells are a traditional woodland flower. Bring the feeling of spring into any room by decorating this harmonious lamp and base.

Paint the bluebell flower heads in different directions to create a more realistic effect.

You will need

Materials

- Lamp base and shade
- Acrylic paint in the following colors: lavender sachet, white, fresh green, dioxide purple, burnt sienna (optional)
- Sponging glaze

Tools

- Fine sandpaper
- Tack cloth
- Tile or palette
- 1-in. flat brush
- Plastic wrap
- ½-in. flat brush
- Filbert brush
- No. 1 liner brush

1 Prepare the surface for painting by sanding it lightly and going over it with a tack cloth. Using the 1-inch flat brush, apply a lavender sachet base coat to the lamp. Don't forget to paint the underside of the base. Leave it to dry.

2 Mix equal parts of white paint and sponging glaze. Brush it on to one side of the lamp base, still using the flat brush. The glaze will make the white seem transparent.

3 Lay plastic wrap on the still-wet paint. Crumble the plastic slightly with your fingers, and press it down to create a textured look. Carefully lift the plastic and let the paint dry. Repeat on all sides.

★★☆ **Skill level**   🕐 **3 hours**   **Techniques:** *Double-loading p. 13*

4 Double-load the ½-inch flat brush with fresh green and white paint. Lead with white and, keeping the brush handle upright, slide the brush on the chisel edge for the stem of the main plant. Working from the stem outwards, leading with the white again, paint the individual bluebell stems.

5 Choose the size of filbert brush to correspond with the size of each bluebell flower. Load the brush with white paint, then side-load both edges with dioxide purple paint. Place the brush at the top of each flower and pull downward, then lift off cleanly. Repeat for the rest of the flowers.

6 Double-load the liner brush with dioxide purple and white paint and make the bluebell frill, as if painting eyelashes. Load the liner with white paint and add tiny highlights to each of the flowers.

7 To paint the leaves, load the ½-inch flat brush with fresh green and white paint. Slide on the chisel edge from the base of the original stem with the white leading. Apply pressure to widen the leaf, lift back to narrow it, repeat, and finish on the chisel edge.

8 For the folded leaf, load the ½-inch flat brush with fresh green and white paint. Start from the base of the central stem of the leaf, sliding the brush and splaying the bristles as you apply pressure to half the length of the leaf. Lift the brush off the surface and reposition with the chisel edge parallel to the leaf. Start the new stroke where the last one finished. With equal pressure, draw the brush downward finishing the stroke on the chisel edge.

9 For an antique finish, apply watered-down burnt sienna paint around the base of the lamp. Wipe off any excess with a damp cloth. Use the same design to decorate the shade.

Helpful hint

For a more dramatic edging effect, rub a little gold gilding cream around any exposed edges. This will make the lamp base more ornate.

Kitchen shelf with acorns

This project has acorns and leaves on a kitchen shelf painted in rich greens and nutty warm browns and is designed to improve your shading and highlighting skills.

Side-loading the brush with floating medium is a great way to shade a project. Use this method whenever you need to create a shaded effect without layering the project.

You will need

Materials
- Kitchen shelf
- Acrylic paint in the following colors: buttercream, evergreen, Hauser green dark, maple syrup
- Tracing paper
- Transfer paper
- Masking tape
- Transparent medium
- Water-based varnish

Tools
- Fine sandpaper
- Tack cloth
- Tile or palette
- 1-in. flat brush
- Pencil or stylus
- ½-in. flat brush
- No. 1 liner brush

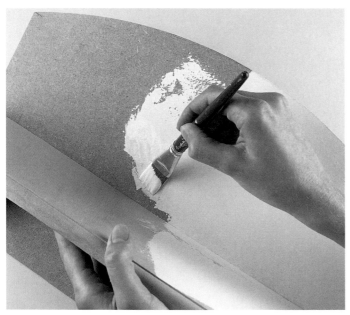

1 Prepare the surface for painting by sanding it lightly and going over it with a tack cloth. Using the 1-inch flat brush, apply a buttercream base coat to the shelf. Leave it to dry.

2 Trace the design on page 77 onto tracing paper, then position the transfer paper between the tracing paper and project. Hold the tracing and transfer papers in place with masking tape and use a pencil or stylus to trace the design.

★★☆ **Skill level**   ⏱ **3 hours**   **Techniques:** *Wiggly leaf p. 14*

3 Double-load a ½-inch flat brush with evergreen and Hauser green dark paint. With the Hauser green dark to the outside, paint the leaves, using two wiggly leaf strokes for each one, working toward the center.

4 Load the ½-inch flat brush with maple syrup paint and apply a base coat to the acorn cups. Double-load the ½-inch flat brush with maple syrup and evergreen paints and make the stems by drawing the brush along the flat of the bristles.

5 Double-load the ½-inch flat brush with maple syrup and buttercream paints and add the acorn nuts.

6 Side-load the ½-inch flat brush with maple syrup paint and transparent medium and shade in the leaves, with the maple syrup to the outside. Reload your brush regularly.

7 Side-load the ½-inch flat brush with evergreen paint and transparent medium and run the brush along the place where the nut joins the cup.

8 Mix white paint with a little water until you have an inklike consistency. Using the liner brush, paint in the lines on the acorn cup. Add a white highlight on the shell. When the project is completely dry, seal it with a coat of varnish. Repeat the steps to paint underneath the shelf if you choose. Paint a green line round the design using the liner brush. Varnish it when dry.

Cabinet with lilies

This small cabinet has been transformed into an elegant piece that will suit any room. The natural look of woodgraining works well with the calla lily design. The lily works equally well whether painted alone or in simple bunches.

Seal the project with water-based acrylic varnish after the graining stage. This will make it possible to wipe off the lily design if you make a mistake.

You will need

Materials
- Cupboard
- Acrylic paint in the following colors: light beige, cream, bayberry, white, butter pecan, yellow ochre
- Sponging glaze
- Water-based varnish

Tools
- Fine sandpaper
- Tack cloth
- Tile or palette
- 1-in. flat brush
- Wood-graining tool
- 3/4-in. flat brush
- 1/2-in. flat brush

1 Prepare the surface for painting by sanding it lightly and going over it with a tack cloth. Using the 1-inch flat brush, apply a light beige base coat to the entire cabinet. Apply two coats, if necessary, and sand lightly between each coat.

Helpful hint
For a professional look, paint the back of the cabinet as well as the interior.

★★☆ **Skill level**   🕐 **3 hours**   **Techniques:** *Flat leaf p. 14*

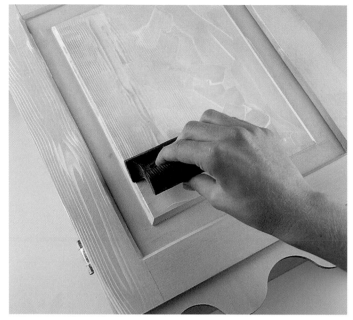

2 Mix equal parts of glaze and cream paint. Apply the mixture to one panel at a time, using random strokes. Start at the top and drag the wood-graining tool down the painted panel, rocking the tool as you go. Wipe off the excess paint before beginning the next panel. Leave it to dry.

3 Paint the stems first because they provide the positioning for the rest of the design. Double-load the 3/4-inch flat brush with bayberry and white paint and make straight strokes with a very sharp chisel edge.

4 To paint the lilies, double-load the 3/4-inch flat brush with white and butter pecan paint. With the white to the outside, push toward the top of the first petal using a flat-leaf stroke. End the stroke by coming up on the chisel edge to complete the petal.

5 Double-load again with butter pecan and white paint for the second stroke. Start where the first stroke ends. Slide the brush on the chisel edge while applying pressure to splay the bristles. Slide back toward the bottom to finish in the middle of the first stroke. Repeat steps 4 and 5 for each of the flowers.

6 This design requires two or three leaf strokes. To paint the green leaves, load the ½-inch flat brush with bayberry and white paint. With the white leading, slide on the chisel edge from the base of the original stem. Apply pressure to splay the bristles and widen the leaf, lift back to the chisel edge to narrow the leaf, and repeat.

7 To finish the flowers, load the ½-inch flat brush with yellow ochre paint. Touch the flower centers with the chisel edge to create stamens.

8 Leave the project to dry. Then seal it with a protective coat of varnish.

Ribbon-and-bow fire screen

Lavender and lilac colors always work well together. This soft faux marble background subtly enhances the timeless ribbons and bows. The effect is impressive and yet easily achieved.

Add a high-gloss varnish finish to a faux marble finish effect to create a realistic look to the design.

You will need

Materials

- Fire screen
- Acrylic paint in the following colors: lavender, lilac, purple, white
- Gel medium
- Gloss varnish

Tools

- Fine sandpaper
- Tack cloth
- Tile or palette
- 1-in. flat brush
- Natural sponge
- Badger brush
- ½-in. flat brush
- No. 1 liner brush
- ¾-in. flat brush

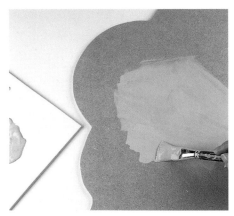

1 Prepare the surface for painting by sanding it lightly and going over it with a soft cloth. Using the 1-inch flat brush, apply a lavender base coat to the screen. Leave it to dry.

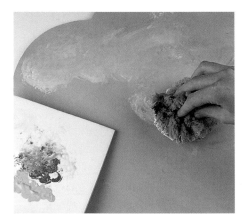

2 Using a dampened sponge, pick up a small amount of lilac paint and gently sponge a random pattern over the painted surface. Occasionally, dip the sponge into a small amount of gel medium. This will keep the paint from drying before it has time to properly bleed.

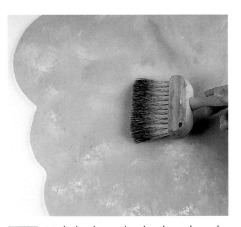

3 Lightly drag the badger brush through the wet paint to soften the sponging.

★★★ **Skill level**   🕐 **3 hours**   **Techniques:** *"C" stroke p. 14*

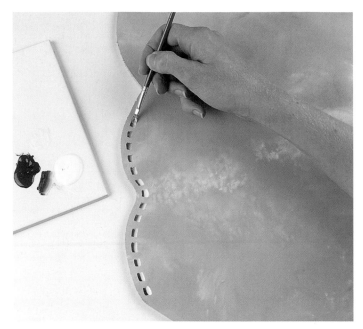

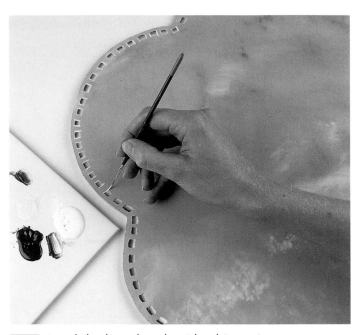

4 Double-load a ½-inch brush with purple and white paint and, following the edge of the fire screen, make short strokes.

5 Load the liner brush with white paint to make lines down the start and finish of the ribbon stroke.

6 To paint the loops of the bow, double-load a ¾-inch brush with purple and white paint. With the purple toward the top of the screen, drag the brush, applying pressure in the direction of the loop. On the return stroke, start to lift the brush so that it finishes on the chisel edge. Repeat the sequence for each of the other loops, re-loading as necessary.

Helpful hint
Use a little of the ribbon colors in the marble background to create a cohesive effect.

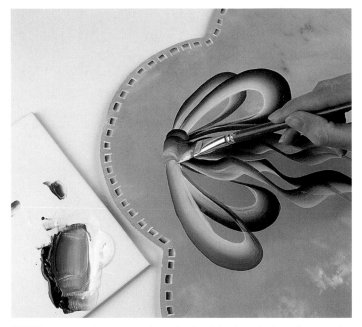

7 Using the same brush double-loaded with purple and white paint, lead with the white to make the ribbon end. Slide the brush toward the base of the fire screen, applying pressure to widen the ribbon. Gently come back up onto the chisel edge of the brush to narrow it. Repeat for each of the ribbon ends.

8 Using the same brush double-loaded with purple and white paint, make two backward "C" strokes on top of each other for the knot of the bow. Leave it to dry and then varnish.

Variation

Decorative waste bin

The design of the ribbon and bow easily adapts to other shapes and surfaces, scaled down it fits perfectly onto this wastepaper basket. The two pieces would work beautifully together to complete any bath or bedroom decor.

Morning-glory corner table

Beautiful trumpet-shaped flowers, delicately intertwined, complement and enhance this corner piece of furniture. A stippled background softens the design while creating a shaded but professional finish.

Morning glories, which grow in any direction, automatically lend themselves to unusual shaped furniture.

You will need

Materials

- Corner table
- Acrylic paint in the following colors: baby blue, night sky, thicket, bayberry, white
- Sponging glaze
- Water-based varnish

Tools

- Fine sandpaper
- Tack cloth
- Tile or palette
- 1-in. flat brush
- Stippling brush
- Clean cloth
- ½-in. flat brush
- No. 1 liner brush

1 Prepare the surface for painting by sanding it lightly and going over it with a tack cloth. Using the 1-inch flat brush, apply a base coat to the table with baby blue paint. Leave it to dry. Mix equal parts of night sky paint and glaze and apply it to the table top.

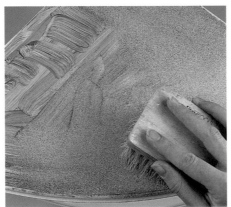

2 While the glaze is still wet, take the stippling brush and pounce from the outer edge toward the center. Continue until you have worked the entire surface and the paint has been dispersed.

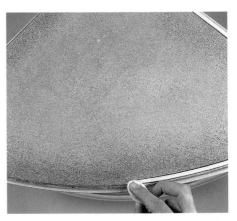

3 Take a clean damp cloth and wipe around the edges of the table to neaten them.

Helpful hint

A damp cloth will give a sharp finish to any glazed edges and is preferable to using masking tape.

★★★ **Skill level**   🕐 **4 hours**   **Techniques:** *Wiggly leaf, Flat leaf p. 14*

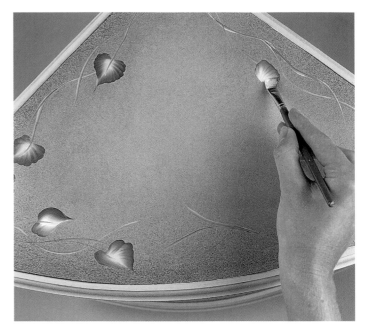

4 Double-load the ½-inch flat brush with thicket and bayberry paint. Create a vine around the outer edge of the stippled area by sliding the brush on the chisel edge. Cross over some of the vines.

5 To paint the leaves, double-load the ½-inch flat brush with thicket and bayberry paint. Start at the base of the leaf with the thicket to the outside. Wiggle the brush up and down while sliding it along the length of the leaf. Repeat for the other side of the leaf, drawing the second stroke into a chisel edge.

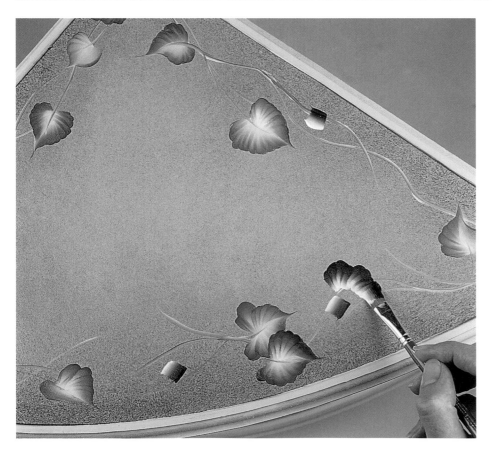

6 To position each of the morning glories, double-load night sky and white paint onto a ½-inch flat brush. Place the brush on the chisel edge and simply slide it, keeping the chisel edge horizontal, for approximately ½ inch. To create the top petal of the trumpet for the morning glory, work from one side of the flower to the other with the brush on the chisel edge and the night sky paint to the top. Wiggle the brush slightly to create indentations in the petals.

7 Starting in the same position as the previous stroke with the night sky to the middle of the trumpet, paint a second petal below the first, joining the base of the flower to the main body.

8 Using the same technique, paint in the small morning glory buds.

9 Double-load the ½-inch flat brush with thicket and bayberry paints, and make the small flat leaves and the leaves at the base of the flower.

Helpful hint

Practise your painting on a piece of acetate; it can be wiped clean and used many times.

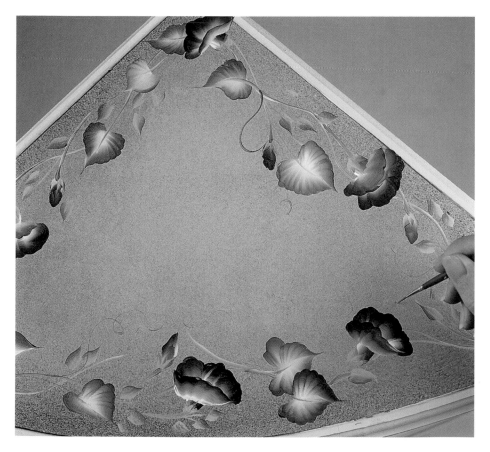

10 Review the design and fill in any blank areas with flat leaves. To paint the tendrils, mix thicket paint with a little water until you have an inklike consistency. Then load the liner brush. Hold the brush above the ferrule, extend your smallest finger to improve balance and paint curly tendrils overlapping each other back and forth in opposite directions. Leave it to dry completely before applying a coat of varnish.

Poppy-painted folding screen

Poppies are always a favorite and I am sure these are no exception. This painting would work perfectly on closet doors, cabinets, or even drawer fronts. Don't forget when putting together designs to include the small elements in the corners.

Paint the corner designs at the same time as the main body of the design. Use a smaller brush to paint these designs.

You will need

Materials

- Hinged wood-panel screen
- Acrylic paint in the following colors: cream, Hauser green dark, yellow ochre, berry wine, bright red, black, thicket, bayberry,
- Water-based varnish

Tools

- Fine sandpaper
- Tack cloth
- Paint roller
- Tile or palette
- ½-in. flat brush
- Small stippling brush
- No. 1 liner brush

1 Prepare the surface for painting by sanding it lightly and going over it with a tack cloth. Use a small paint roller to apply a base coat to the panels with cream paint. Apply two coats, if necessary. Leave to dry between coats.

2 Load the ½-inch flat brush with Hauser green dark and yellow ochre paints and make the vine as an oval in the center of the screen. Re-load where necessary, keeping the chisel edge sharp at all times.

★★★ **Skill level**   🕐 **4 hours**   **Techniques:** *Wiggly leaf p. 14*

3 Use the photograph on page 73 as a guide for the positioning of each of the poppies. Double-load berry wine and bright red paints onto a ½-inch flat brush. Paint the top petal of the poppy, working from one side of the flower to the other with the brush on the chisel edge and the bright red to the top. Wiggle the brush slightly to create indentations in the petals.

Helpful hint
A tiny amount of red paint on the brush adds an interesting color accent to the wiggly leaves.

4 Starting in the same position as the previous stroke, with the berry wine to the middle of the petal, paint a second petal below the first, joining the two petals on either side. Vary the size of the strokes.

5 Double-load a small stippling brush with black and yellow ochre paints. With the yellow ochre to the top of the petal, position the stamen in the center of the flower.

6 Stand back from the design and add more vines if necessary.

7 To paint the leaves, double-load the ½-inch flat brush with thicket and bayberry paints. Start at the base of the leaf on the chisel edge of the brush, with the thicket to the outside of the leaf. Apply pressure and wiggle the brush up and down while sliding it along the length of the leaf. Repeat the process for the bottom of the leaf, carefully drawing the second stroke into a sharp chisel edge. For variety, alternate the colors, using yellow ochre instead of bayberry.

8 To paint the tendrils, mix thicket paint with a little water until you have an inklike consistency, then load the liner brush. Hold the brush above the ferrule, extend the smallest finger to improve balance, and paint loops overlapping each other back and forth in opposite directions, around the oval. Before varnishing the project, stand back from the design and add any further petals if required.

Templates

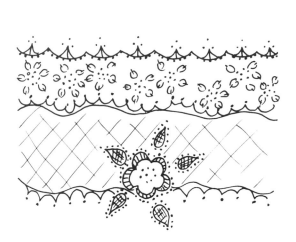

↑ **Lace tissue box (pages 16–19)**
Set photocopier to 133% to enlarge the image to the correct size for project.

← **Rooster message board (pages 36–39)**
Set photocopier to 133% to enlarge the image to the correct size for project.

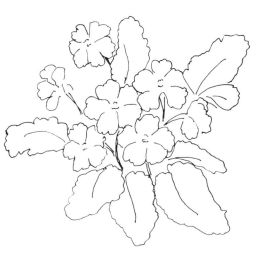

↑ **Primrose cachepot (pages 28–31)**
Set photocopier to 200% to enlarge the image to the correct size for project.

← **Neoclassical wall cabinet (pages 24–27)** Set photocopier to 133% to enlarge the image to the correct size for project.

← **Plum-and-plum-leaf tray (pages 48–51)** Set photocopier to 133% to enlarge the image to the correct size for project.

← **Kitchen shelf with acorns (pages 56–59)** Set photocopier to 200% to enlarge the image to the correct size for project.

Suppliers

USA

Ampersand Art Supply
1500 E. 4th St.
Austin, TX 78702
(800) 822-1939
www.ampersand.com

Acme Sponge & Chamois Co.
P.O. Box 339
Tarpon Springs, FL 34688
(727) 937-3222
www.acmesponge.com

Arnold Grummer's
830 N. 109th, Suite 1
Wauwatosa. WI 53226
(800) 453-1485
www.arnoldgrummer.com

Arts & Crafts by Rayson
720 S. Dickerson St.
Burgaw, NC 28425
(800) 526-1526
www.artsandcraftsbyrason.com

Binney & Smith, Inc.
1100 Church Lane
Easton, PA 18044
(800) 272-9652
www.binney-smith.com

Canvas Concepts
(800) 869-7220
www.canvasconcepts.com

Chroma
205 Bucky Dr.
Lititz, PA 17543
(717) 626-8826
www.chromaonline.com

ColArt America, Inc.
11 Constitution Way
Piscataway, NJ 08855
(800) 445-4278
www.winsornewton.com

Colker Co.
2618 Penn Ave.
Pittsburgh, PA 15222
(800) 533-6561
www.colkercompany.com

Daler-Rowney USA
2 Corporate Dr.
Cranbury, NJ 08512
(609) 655-5252
www.daler-rowney.com

Da Vinci Paint Co.
11 Good Year St.
Irvine, CA 92618
(949) 859-4890
www.davincipaints.com

Delta Paints and Coatings
2550 Pellissier Place
Whittier, CA 90601
(800) 423-4135
www.deltaonline.com

Duncan
5673 E. Shields Avenue
Fresno, CA 93727
(800) 438-6226
www.duncan-enterprises.com

Fe Fi Faux
(805) 968-1905
www.fefifaux.com

Grumbacher
(800) 323-0749
(800) 668-4575 in Canada
www.sanford.com

Houston Art, Inc.
10770 Moss Ridge Rd.
Houston, TX 77043
(800) 272-3804
www.houstonart.com

J.W. Etc
2205 First St., Suite 103
Simi Valley, CA 93065
(805) 526-5066
www.jwetc.com

Loew-Cornell
563 Chestnut Ave.
Teaneck, NJ 07666
(201) 836-8110
www.loew-cornell.com

Palmer Paint Products
1291 Rochester Rd.
Troy, MI 48083
(800) 521-1383
www.palmerpaint.com

Plaid Industries
P.O. Box 7600
Norcross, GA 30091
(800) 842-4197
www.plaidonline.com

Solo Horton Brushes
P.O. Box 478
Winsted, CT 06098
(800) 969-7656
www.solobrushes.com

Symphony Faux Finishing Tools
1201 Jackson St.
Philadelphia, PA 19148
(800) 523-9095
www.besttliebco.com

T.J. Ronan Paint Corp.
749 E. 135th St.
Bronx, NY 10454
(800) 654-3640
www.ronanpaints.com

U.S. Art Quest
7800 Ann Arbor Rd.
Grass Lake, MI 49240
(517) 522-6225
www.usartquest.com

Zinsser
173 Belmont Dr.
Somerset, NJ 08875
(732) 469-8100
www.zinsser.com

CANADA

General Paint
950 Raymur Ave.
Vancouver, BC V6A 3C5
(888) 301-4454
www.generalpaint.com

Laurentide, Inc.
10 010, Rue Mirabeau
Ville d'Anjou
Montreal, QC G9N 6T5
(800) 361-3892
www.societelaurentide.com

Nour Trading Company
637 Colby Dr.
Waterloo, ON N2V 1B4
(800) 686-6687
www.nour.com

Para Paints
11 Kenview Blvd.
Bampton, ON L6T 5G5
(905) 792-0940
www.para.com

ASSOCIATIONS

USA

American Craft Council
21 S. Eltings Corner Rd.
Highland, NY 12528
(800) 836-3470
www.craftcouncil.org

**Arts and Crafts Association of
America**
4888 Cannon Woods Ct.
Belmont, MI 49306
(616) 874-1721
www.artsandcraftsassoc.com

**Association of Crafts & Creative
Industries**
1100-H Brandywine Blvd.
P.O. Box 3388
Zanesville, OH 43702
(740) 452-4541
www.accicrafts.org

Hobby Industry Association
319 E. 54th St.
Elmwood Park, NJ 07407
(201) 794-1133
www.hobby.org

National Craft Association
1945 E. Ridge Rd., Suite 5178
Rochester, NY 14622
(800) 715-9594

CANADA

Canada Craft and Hobby Association
24 1410-40 Ave,. N.E.
Calgary, AL T2E 6L1
(403) 291-0559

Canadian Carfts Federation
c/o Ontario Crafts Council
Designers Walk
170 Bedford Rd., Suite 300
Toronto, ON M5R 2K9
(416) 408-2294
www.canadiancraftsfederation.ca

Index

acetate sheets, 10
acorns, kitchen shelf with, 56–59
acrylic paints, 9
acrylic sealant, 10

backgrounds: faux marble, 64–67
  smoke marbling, 28, 31
  stippling, 68–69
  wood-graining, 60–62
bluebell lamp and shade, 52–55
boxes: bumble bee jewelry box, 40–43
  lace tissue box, 16–19
  memory box, 19
  Victorian jewelry box, 35
brush basins, 10
brushes, 8–9
  painting techniques, 13–15
bumble bee: bumble bee candles, 43
  jewelry box with, 40–43

"C" strokes, 14–15
cabinets: cabinet with lilies, 60–63
  Neoclassical wall cabinet, 24–27
cachepot, primrose, 28–31
candles, bumble bee, 43
cleaning brushes, 8–9
clock, kitchen, 39
color mixing, 15
colors, 9
crackle glaze, 32–35

double-loading brushes, 13

equipment and materials, 8–11

faux marble effect, 64–65
  smoke marbling, 28, 31
fern motif: framed painting, 23
  kitchen utensil holder, 20–23

filbert brushes, 8
fire screen, ribbons and bows, 64–67
flat brushes, 8
  loading, 13
flat-leaf strokes, 14
flogger brushes, 8
flower motifs, 15
  bluebell lamp and shade, 52–55
  cabinet with lilies, 60–63
  floral pegged rack, 32–35
  poppy-painted folding screen, 72–75
  primrose cachepot, 28–31
  smoke-marbled roses, 31
  Victorian jewelry box, 35
framed painting, 23
fruit motif, plums and plum leaves tray, 48–51

glazes: crackle glaze, 32–5
  scumble glaze, 10
gold leaf, 10
  plum-and-plum-leaf tray, 48–51

herb motifs: painted herb pots, 44–47
  lazy Susan herbs, 47

jewelry boxes, 35, 40–43

kitchen clock, 39
kitchen shelf with acorns, 56–59
kitchen utensil holder, 20–23

lace tissue box, 16–19
lamp, bluebell, 52–55
lazy Susan herbs, 47
leaf motifs: painted herb pots, 44–47
  kitchen shelf with acorns, 56–59

kitchen utensil holder, 20–23
  lazy Susan herbs, 47
  plums and plum leaves tray, 48–51
lilies, cabinet with, 60–63
line strokes, 14
liner brushes, 8
loading brushes, 13

materials and equipment, 8–11
MDF (medium density fiberboard), 12
memory box, 19
message board, rooster, 36–39
mixing colors, 15
morning-glory corner table, 68–71

Neoclassical wall cabinet, 24–27
painted folding screen, poppy, 72–75
painted pots, herb, 44–47
painting, framed, 23
paints, 9
  loading brushes, 13
  stripping paint, 15
  techniques, 13–15
palettes, 10
paper towels, 10
pegged rack, floral, 32–35
pigments, 9
plum-and-plum-leaf tray, 48–51
plywood, 12
poppy-painted folding screen, 72–75
preparation, 12
primary colors, 9
primrose cachepot, 28–31

ribbons and bows fire screen, 64–67
rooster message board, 36–39
rooster motif: message board, 36–39

kitchen clock, 39
roses, smoke marbled, 31
round brushes, 8
  loading, 14

sanding wood surfaces, 15
sandpaper, 10
scumble glaze, 10
sealant, acrylic, 10
shelf with acorns, 56–59
side-loading brushes, 13
smoke marbling, 28, 31
sponges, 10
steel wool, 10
stippling, 68
stippling brushes, 8
stripping paint, 15
strokes, painting techniques, 14–15
surfaces, 12
swirls, 15

table, morning-glory, 68–71
tack cloths, 10
techniques, 13–15
templates, 76–77
tendrils, 15
terra cotta: herb painted pots, 44–47
  preparation, 12
tipping, 14
tracing paper, 10
transfer paper, 10
tray, plums and plum leaves, 48–51

utensil holder, 20–23

varnish, 10, 15
Victorian jewelry box, 35

wastepaper basket, decorative, 67
wiggly leaf strokes, 14
wood, preparation, 12, 15
woodgraining, 10, 60–62